21st Century Junior Library

Brachiosaurus

by Josh Gregory

CHERRY LAKE PUBLISHING * ANN ARBOR, MICHIGAN

CHERRY LAKE
Publishing

Published in the United States of America by Cherry Lake Publishing
Ann Arbor, Michigan
www.cherrylakepublishing.com

Content Adviser: Gregory M. Erickson, PhD, Paleontologist, Department of Biological Science, Florida State University, Tallahassee, Florida

Reading Adviser: Marla Conn, Read With Me Now

Photo Credits: Cover and pages 10 and 14, © Elenarts/Shutterstock.com; pages 4 and 6, © Catmando/Shutterstock.com; page 8, © Kostyantyn Ivanyshen/Shutterstock.com; page 12, © Sofia Santos/Shutterstock.com, page 16, © Bob Orsillo/Shutterstock.com; page 18, © Michael Rosskothen/Shutterstock.com; James St. John / tinyurl.com/q8uk8mk / CC-BY-2.0.

LIBRARY OF CONGRESS CATALOGING-IN-PUBLICATION DATA
Gregory, Josh, author.
  Brachiosaurus / by Josh Gregory.
      pages cm.—(Dinosaurs) (21st century junior library)
  Summary: "Learn about dinosaur known as Brachiosaurus, from what it ate to how it lived."—Provided by publisher.
  Audience: K to grade 3.
  Includes bibliographical references and index.
  ISBN 978-1-63362-381-1 (lib. bdg.)—ISBN 978-1-63362-409-2 (pbk.)—
ISBN 978-1-63362-437-5 (pdf)—ISBN 978-1-63362-465-8 (e-book)
  1. Brachiosaurus—Juvenile literature. 2. Dinosaurs—Juvenile literature. I. Title.
QE862.S3G7667 2016
567.913—dc23   2014045646

Cherry Lake Publishing would like to acknowledge the work of
The Partnership for 21st Century Skills.
Please visit www.p21.org for more information.

Printed in the United States of America
Corporate Graphics
July 2015

CONTENTS

Brachiosaurus was one of the largest
land animals on Earth.

What Was Brachiosaurus?

Long ago, a huge dinosaur called *Brachiosaurus* lived on Earth. It was very tall. Other dinosaurs could have walked between its legs! This giant **reptile** roamed the forests of North America and Africa. A *Brachiosaurus* might have walked through what is now your backyard!

Experts think *Brachiosaurus* lived in groups called herds.

Brachiosaurus lived between 156 million and 147 million years ago. You won't find one living today. Like all dinosaurs, it is **extinct**. We know about dinosaurs from **fossils** of their bones. Scientists study these objects to learn how these **prehistoric** reptiles lived.

Ask Questions!

Why do you think the dinosaurs went extinct? Scientists have some ideas about why this happened. Look for information in books or on Web sites. Ask your teachers to help you.

Brachiosaurus's tail was short compared to its long neck.

What Did *Brachiosaurus* Look Like?

Brachiosaurus looked a lot like a huge giraffe. It had a very long neck and a small head. The neck connected to a heavy, round body. Most of the dinosaur's weight was in the front. The back of its body led to a small tail.

Brachiosaurus had strong legs to
hold its heavy body.

Brachiosaurus's legs were round like tree trunks. Its front legs were longer than its back legs. Its feet looked like those of an elephant. Each foot had a soft pad in the middle. This cushioned the dinosaur's heavy steps. Its toes came around the sides of the pad.

Brachiosaurus was much bigger than an
adult human is today.

Brachiosaurus was one of the largest dinosaurs ever to live. With its neck stretched high, it reached a height of around 40 feet (12 meters). That is about the height of a four-story building! It weighed more than 110,000 pounds (50,000 kilograms). That is the weight of a fully loaded semi truck!

Create!

Now you have an idea what *Brachiosaurus* looked like. But how do you think the dinosaur moved? What kind of poses could it make? Try drawing some *Brachiosaurus* pictures of your own. How do they look?

Brachiosaurus could rise onto its back legs if it needed to. This allowed it to reach higher.

How Did
Brachiosaurus Live?

Brachiosaurus ate plants. Scientists think it used its long neck to reach leaves at the top of trees. This dinosaur probably spent its time searching for food and eating. Because its body was so huge, it needed a lot of food.

Brachiosaurus did not have any wide grinding teeth for chewing its food.

Brachiosaurus had 52 teeth. These teeth were curved like spoons. The dinosaur used them to pull mouthfuls of leaves from branches. The dinosaur did not chew its food. Instead, its tongue pushed food to the back of its mouth. Then the dinosaur swallowed everything whole.

Brachiosaurus had a good view of its
surroundings from high above.

Brachiosaurus had to keep an eye out for **predators**. Its long neck may have helped with this. Even when it was eating, the dinosaur could see above the treetops. It could spot enemies from far away. This gave it more time to get away. It needed as much time as possible. *Brachiosaurus* was not a fast runner!

A copy of a *Brachiosaurus*'s bones stands outside the Field Museum in Chicago, Illinois.

People discovered the first *Brachiosaurus* fossils in the early 1900s. Many more have been found since then. However, there is still a lot to learn about this amazing creature. Are you interested in studying dinosaurs? Maybe you will make the next big *Brachiosaurus* discovery!

Look!

You can see fossils for yourself by visiting a museum. Talk to your parents or a teacher. Ask if you can visit a museum with *Brachiosaurus* fossils. A closer look will show you just how big this dinosaur was!

GLOSSARY

extinct (ek-STINGKT) describing a type of plant or animal that has completely died out

fossils (FAH-suhlz) the preserved remains of living things from thousands or millions of years ago

predators (PRED-uh-turz) animals that live by hunting other animals for food

prehistoric (pree-his-TOR-ik) belonging to a time before history was recorded in written form

reptile (REP-tile) a cold-blooded, scaly animal that usually reproduces by laying eggs

FIND OUT MORE

BOOKS

Lindeen, Carol. *Brachiosaurus*. Mankato, MN: Capstone Press, 2006.

Nunn, Daniel. *Brachiosaurus*. Chicago: Heinemann Library, 2015.

Rockwood, Leigh. *Brachiosaurus*. New York: PowerKids Press, 2012.

WEB SITES

KidsDinos—Brachiosaurus

www.kidsdinos.com /dinosaurs-for-children .php?dinosaur=Brachiosaurus
Visit this site for a lot more facts, and follow links to learn more about other dinosaurs, too.

Walking with Dinosaurs—Brachiosaurus

www.dinosaurlive.com /dinosaurs/brachiosaurus
Check out pictures, facts, and a video about this giant prehistoric animal.

INDEX

ABOUT THE AUTHOR

Josh Gregory writes and edits books for kids. He lives in Chicago, Illinois.